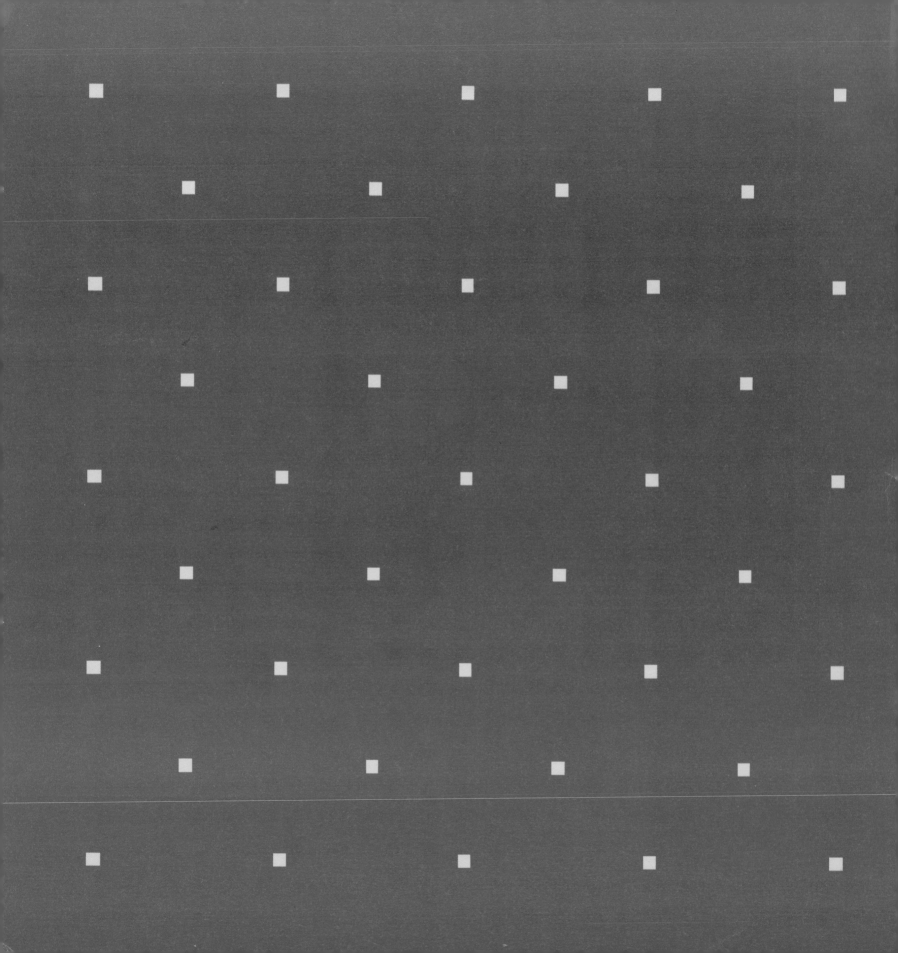

To David, Dylan, and Joey, with special thanks to Mom and Dad.

ISBN 0-590-60713-8

Copyright © 1993 by Kathleen Fain.
All rights reserved.
Published by Scholastic Inc., 555 Broadway, New York, NY 10012, by arrangement with Chronicle Books.

12 11 10 9 8 7 6 5 4 3 2   5 6 7 8 9/9

Printed in the U.S.A.   08

First Scholastic printing, September 1994

Kathleen Fain

HANDSIGNS

A Sign Language Alphabet

Scholastic Inc.
New York Toronto London Auckland Sydney

Aa

Bb

Cc

Dd

Ee

Zz

Yy

Xx

A Note on American Sign Language

American Sign Language (ASL) is the fourth most-used language in the United States (behind English, Spanish, and Italian). It is used by a variety of people, primarily the hearing impaired. Other people who sometimes use ASL to communicate clearly and effectively without the use of words are police officers, rescue teams, and people participating in underwater activities such as scuba diving.

ASL has its own unique vocabulary and grammar, and just as the English language is constantly evolving, so, too, does ASL evolve. New signs are constantly being created and the signs for various words may vary from region to region.

The most basic element of ASL is the American Manual Alphabet. Each letter of the alphabet is represented by a different handsign, which can be used to spell out words. This is called "finger spelling."

The purpose of this book is to teach the American Manual Alphabet—the foundation of manual speech—so that you can begin to communicate by finger spelling. All of the images in this book are accompanied by the letter-sign representing the first letter in the name of the animal being portrayed. For instance, the sign on the cover of this book represents the letter "B." In order to convey "bear," you would need to sign the four letters (B-E-A-R) that make up the animal's name.

When learning to finger spell, it is best to start with smaller words and then progress to longer ones. As you finger spell a word, try to keep each letter sign distinct from the others, and slowly mouth the word (not the individual letters) as you spell it. Using finger spelling, you can sign all the animals in this book, send "secret" messages to your friends, and, most importantly, communicate with the hearing impaired.

Ww

Vv

Uu

Tt

Ss

Ff

Gg
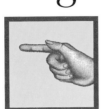

Hh

Ii

Jj
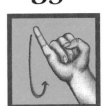

Kk

Ll

Mm

A Short History of Manual Speech

16th century — Geronimo Cardano, an Italian physician, asserted that the deaf could be taught to understand written communication by associating written symbols with the objects or actions they represented.

1620 — A manual alphabet was published for the first time.

1755 — Abbé Charles Michel de L'Epée of Paris established the first free school for the deaf. Drawing on a system of signs already being used by a group of deaf Parisians, he created a signed version of spoken French.

1778 — In Germany, Samuel Heinicke founded the first school for the deaf to receive government recognition.

1817 — After returning from a European tour, Thomas Hopkins Gallaudet, a minister interested in helping a young deaf neighbor, founded the first school for the deaf in the United States.

1864 — Gallaudet College, still the only liberal arts college for the deaf in the world, was founded in Washington D.C.

Today — American Sign Language (ASL) is used by approximately two million people in the United States.

Rr

Qq

Pp

Oo

Nn

Aa

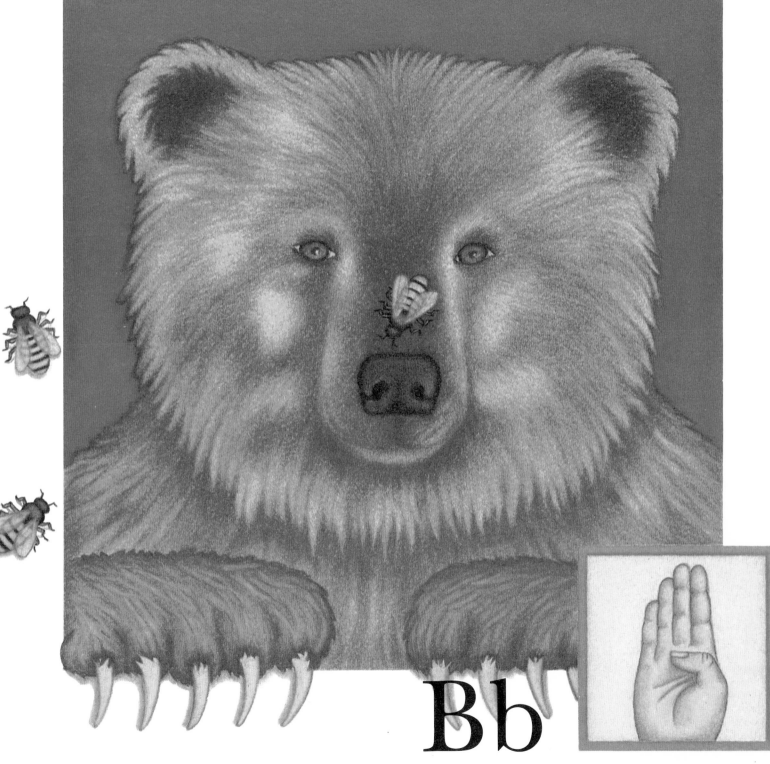

Bb

Cc

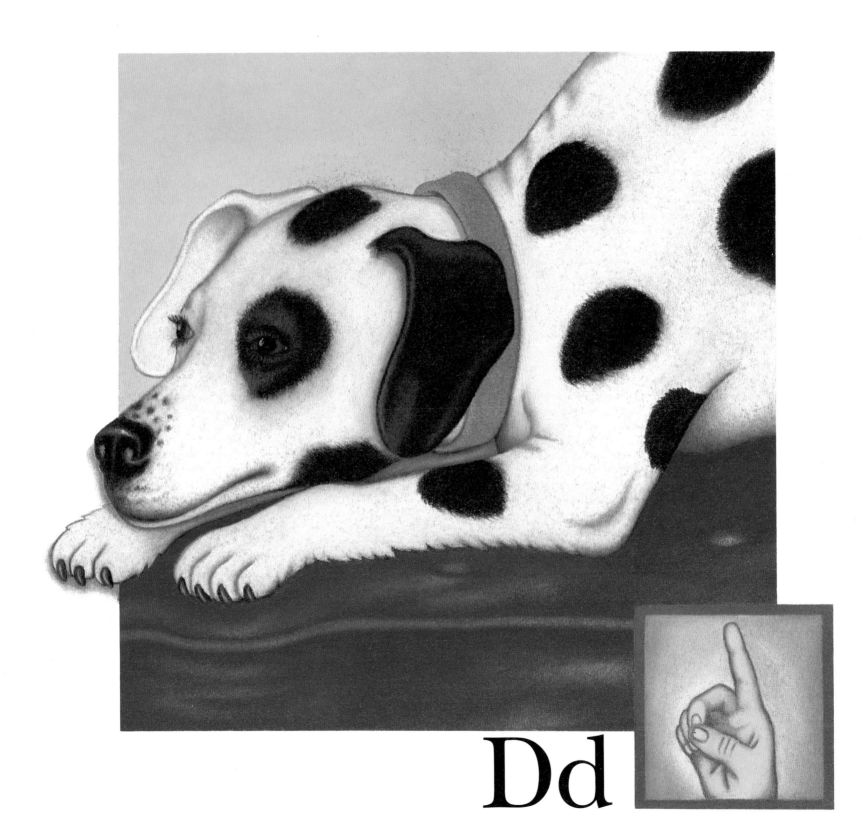

Dd

Ee

Ff

Gg

Hh

Ii

Jj

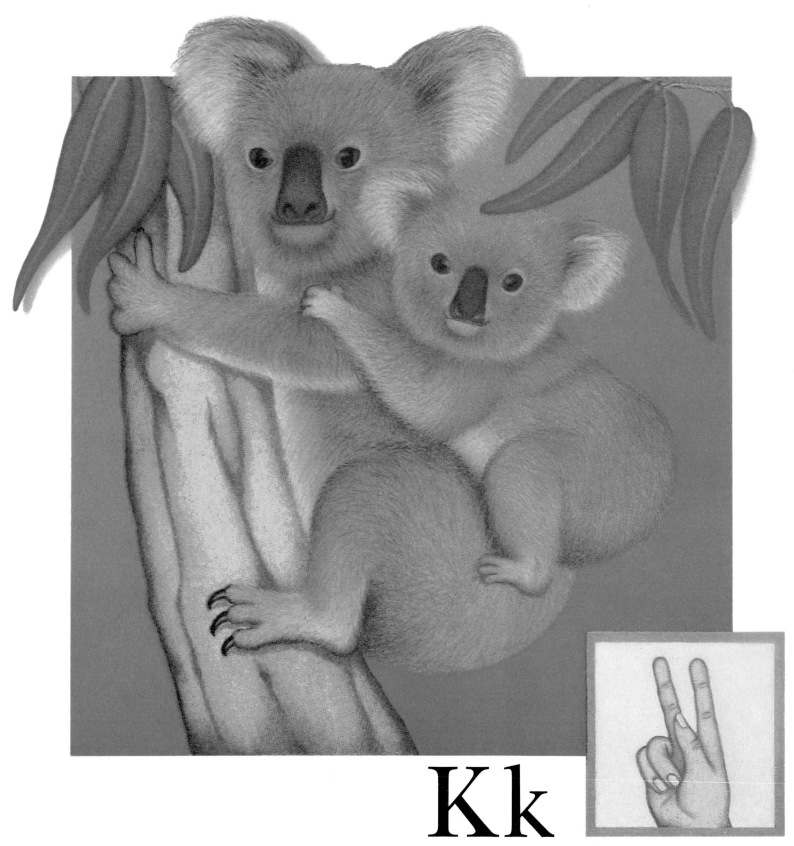

Kk

Ll

Mm

Nn

Oo

Pp

Qq

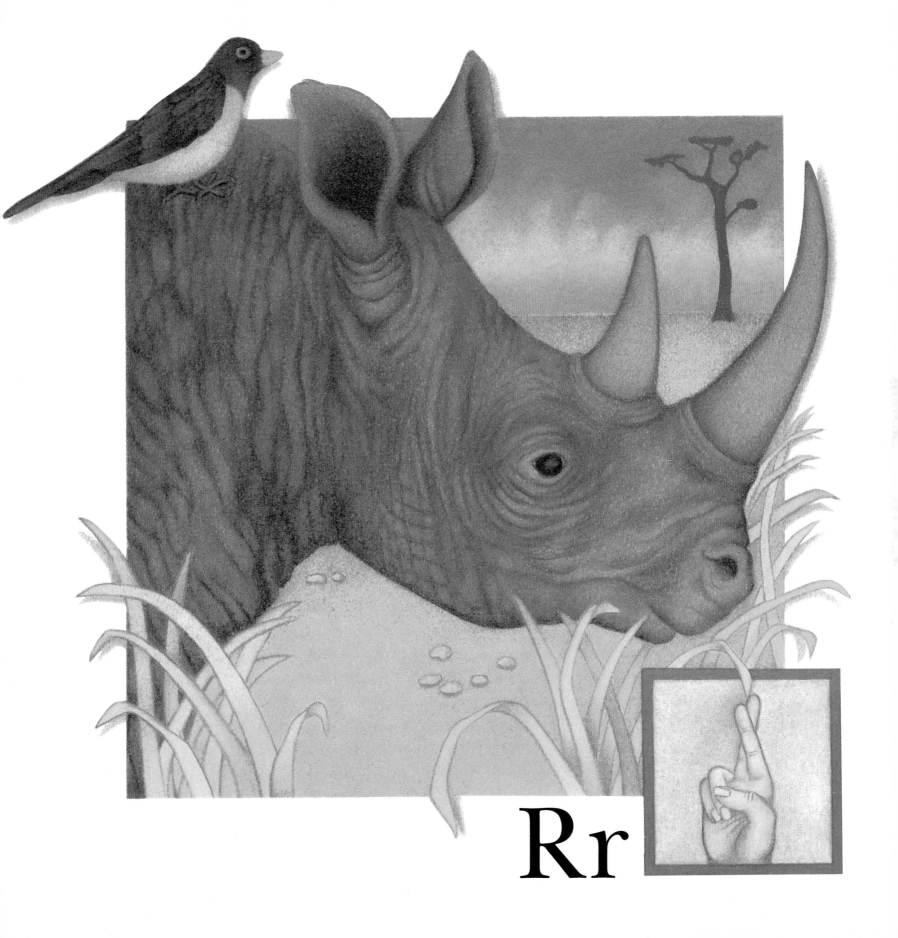

Rr

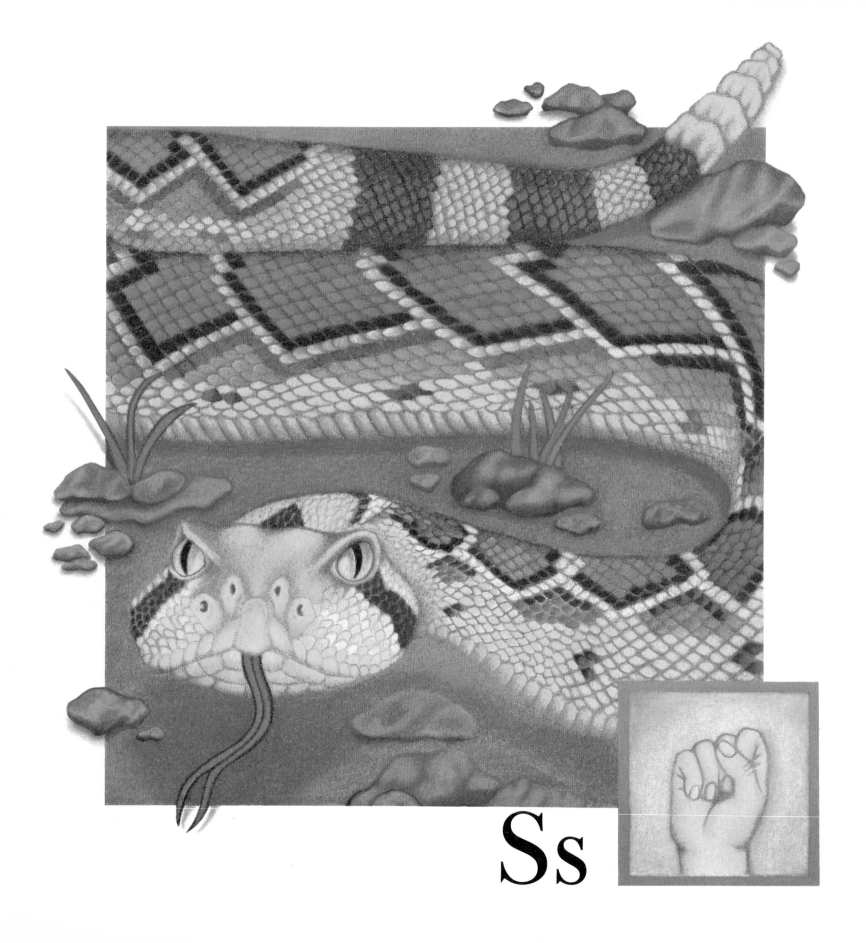

Ss

Tt

Uu

Vv

Ww

Xx

Yy

Zz

GLOSSARY OF ANIMALS

Anteater
Anteaters are found in South and Central America. They have no teeth, so they must lap up their prey with their long, sticky tongues. They feed on all kinds of insects, although they generally prefer ants and termites. Anteaters don't build burrows or nests, but sleep in the open, wrapping their hairy tails around them like a blanket.

Bear
There are many species of bear. Members of the northern family include the American Black Bear, the grizzly bear, the brown bear, and the polar bear. Bears are carnivorous mammals, but, unlike most carnivores, they eat plants as well as meat. Although some bears can stand as tall as ten feet and can weigh as much as 1,500 pounds, when they are first born they weigh about one pound.

Cow
Cows are one of the most familiar farm animals. From a cow's milk we get the milk we drink, as well as cream, butter, and ice cream.

Dog
While the ancestry of dogs is still uncertain, it is certain that domesticated dogs have been around for as long as 10,000 years. Many believe that dogs descended from wolves, while others believe that they may have descended from a now extinct ancestor. Today, there are more than 100 breeds of domestic dogs. The largest is the St. Bernard, which can weigh as much as 200 pounds. The smallest is the Chihuahua, which can weigh as little as two pounds.

Elephant
Elephants can grow to be as tall as eleven feet high and weigh up to six tons, making them the largest living land animals. Elephants travel in herds, sleep standing up, and may live to be as old as 70 years. While there used to be many different species of elephant, including the now extinct mammoths and mastodons, today only two species remain: the African elephant and the Asian elephant.

Flamingo
Different species of flamingo can be found in the Americas, southern Europe, South and East Africa, and India. They are even found high in the Andean mountains, home of the rare James's flamingo. Flamingos are famous for their bright coloring and unusual shape.

Giraffe
Giraffes are the world's tallest animal: a male may stand as tall as 18 feet high. Their long necks allow them to graze on the leaves of trees. Giraffes can be found in the savannas of Africa, south of the Sahara Desert. They can go for long periods without drinking or sleeping. In fact, some biologists believe that giraffes do not sleep at all. When baby giraffes, or calves, are born, they are about six feet tall and weigh over 100 pounds.

Hawk
Hawks are members of the raptor group, which also includes eagles and owls. Raptors are birds of prey that have hooked upper beaks, excellent vision, and feet with sharp claws called talons. Hawks feed on all kinds of animals, such as mice, rabbits, squirrels, snakes, lizards, and other birds.

Iguana

The iguana family contains more than 700 different species, making it one of the largest groups of lizards. Land iguanas live in the warm parts of North and South America. The green iguana can grow to be six feet long. Its green coloration camouflages it well in its leafy tropical forest home. Green iguanas live in Central and Southern America where they eat shoots, fruits, flowers, and leaves. The marine iguana is the only marine lizard that swims and feeds in the sea. A large, greenish-brown lizard, the iguana is a territorial reptile that fiercely defends itself against rivals.

Jackrabbit

Jackrabbits are actually not rabbits at all, but hares. Hares have bigger ears and longer legs than rabbits, and, unlike baby rabbits, hares are born with their eyes open and can hop immediately after birth. Jackrabbits can be found in the arid desert areas of the western United States. They seldom drink, getting all the moisture they need from plants. Their long ears help them to keep cool by giving off heat and to detect enemies. They use their strong hind legs to bound away from danger, reaching speeds of up to 45 miles per hour.

Koala

Koalas are only found in Australia, where they live in the eucalyptus trees that provide their favorite food: eucalyptus leaves. Although they are commonly referred to as "koala bears," the koala is not a bear at all, but a marsupial. The name "koala" comes from an Aboriginal word meaning "no drink," for koalas get all the moisture they need from their food.

Lynx

Lynx are members of the cat family. The European lynx lives in northern Europe and Asia, the Spanish lynx in southern Europe, and the Canadian lynx in North America. Lynx generally live in pine forests where they hunt at night for hares, rabbits, birds, fish, and small deer.

Moose

Moose are the largest members of the deer family. They stand nearly eight feet tall and the male's antlers can span more than six feet. Moose live in the wooded areas of Canada, Maine, Alaska, Minnesota, Wisconsin, and the Rocky Mountains, as well as in Norway, Sweden, Russia, Mongolia, and northern China. They can live to be 20 years old.

Nautilus

There are six species of nautilus, all of which are found in the southwest Pacific Ocean. The nautilus is a celaphod, like octopi and squid, but unlike other members of this class it has an external shell. The nautilus is able to swim, and uses its tentacles to grip fish and other animals for food.

Octopus

There are 150 different species of octopus. They can be found in every sea in the world, but are most common in warm waters. Octopi usually swim backwards, which they accomplish by blowing water through a tube called a siphon.

Parrot

There are 317 species of parrot, almost all of which live in the tropical forests of Australia, Central America, and South America. They are social, noisy animals, and their ability to imitate sounds has made them popular pets. In the wild, they generally live in nests built in tree cavities, although some species will build burrows in the ground or in rock crevices. The parrot featured in this book is a scarlet macaw, which lives in Panama and Costa Rica.

Quail

There are nearly 100 species of quail, all of which belong to the pheasant family. They live in fields, in small family groups called coveys, and rarely leave the ground unless forced to fly. Quail eat seeds, insects, and small snails.

Rhinoceros

The rhinoceros is a hooved mammal related to the horse, and can be easily identified by the horn (or in some cases, horns) that are found on its snout. There are five species of rhinoceros, all of which live in Asia or Africa. They can grow to be over six feet tall and weigh up to four tons. Because of hunting, the rhinoceros is in serious danger of extinction.

Rhinoceros are often seen with small birds called **Oxpeckers**. These birds eat the ticks that live in the rhinoceros's hide.

Snake

There are 2,300 different species of snake, and they can be found on every continent except Antarctica. Some snakes live in burrows, others on the ground and others in trees or water. Snakes have excellent vision, but they cannot hear: they use their tongues to "sense" their surroundings and to help them in hunting, as well as to avoid predators. Most snakes lay eggs, although a few species, such as the rattlesnake, do give birth to live young. Only 300 species of snake are dangerous to humans. These snakes hold venom in their front fangs and their bites can be fatal. Rattlesnakes are named for the rattle found at the tip of their tails.

Tortoise

Tortoises are reptiles whose bodies are protected by a shell into which they can withdraw their legs and heads. They have changed little since they first started evolving 200 million years ago. Land tortoises are amongst the longest-living animals in the world. One tortoise reputedly lived to be more than 200 years old. Most species of tortoise live in the warmer parts of the world. They lay their eggs in holes dug into sandy beaches and allow the sun's heat to help their eggs hatch.

Urchin

The urchin is an invertebrate animal that lives in the sea and is a member of the echinoderm family. It is preyed upon by many ocean animals, such as the sea otter.

Vixen

A vixen is a female fox. The fox is a member of the dog family, and foxes can be found in Asia, Europe, and North America. They feed mainly on rodents, but supplement their diet with birds, frogs, and plants. In the springtime, a vixen generally gives birth to a litter of three to eight cubs.

Wolf

There are several species of wolf, including the red wolf, the arctic wolf, the timber wolf, and the gray wolf. Wolves can be found in North America, Europe, and Asia. They generally live in groups, or packs, which allows them to work together to hunt larger animals and to care for their young.

Xenosaur

Xenosaurus is a species of the Xenosauridae (or "crocodile lizard") family. Xenosaurs live in Central America and southern China. They are nocturnal lizards and are rarely seen. Xenosaurs eat insects, and live mainly under tree roots and in rocky crevices. The female generally gives birth to litters of three live young—each of which measures just over an inch in length.

Yak

The wild yak can only be found in Tibet. The male yak, or bull, can stand as tall as six feet, weigh nearly a ton, and has horns that can span as much as three feet. Generally, the bulls live alone or in small groups of up to five males. Female yaks and their calves live together in herds of anywhere from 20 to 200 animals.

Zebra

The zebra is a member of the equidae family and is related to the horse. There are three species of zebra, but the most common is the Burchell's zebra, which lives in Africa between Namibia and the Sudan.